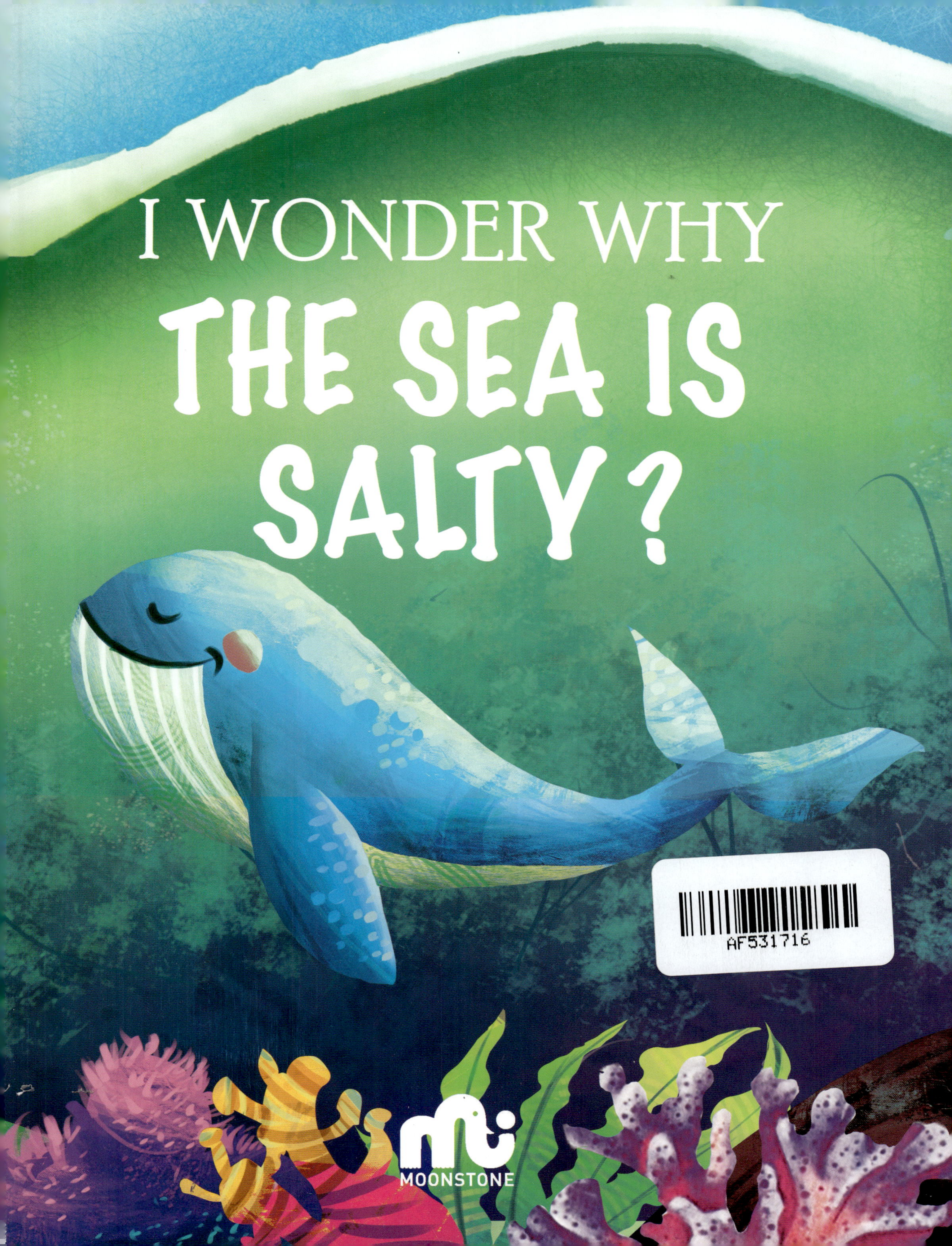
I WONDER WHY
THE SEA IS SALTY?
MOONSTONE

PUBLISHED IN MOONSTONE
BY RUPA PUBLICATIONS INDIA PVT. LTD 2026
161-B/4, GULMOHAR HOUSE,
YUSUF SARAI COMMUNITY CENTRE,
NEW DELHI 110049

SALES CENTRES:
BENGALURU CHENNAI
HYDERABAD KOLKATA MUMBAI

P-ISBN: 978-93-7003-517-1
E-ISBN: 978-93-7003-441-9

FIRST IMPRESSION 2026

10 9 8 7 6 5 4 3 2 1

PRINTED IN INDIA

Table Of Contents

Whyt Is The Sea Salty ?

Did someone pour salt into the sea ?

NOPE! NO GIANT SALT SHAKER WAS FEVER DUMPED IN. BUT IT'S A GREAT QUESTION– BECAUSE THE SEA REALLY DOES TASTE SALTY (JUST ASK YOUR TONGUE). THAT SALT HAS BEEN SLOWLY COLLECTING IN THE SEA OVER MILLIONS OF YEARS.

So where did the salt come from ?

FROM THE LAND! WHEN IT RAINS, THE WATER WEARS DOWN ROCKS–VERY, VERY SLOWLY. BITS OF MINERALS AND SALT GET WASHED INTO RIVERS AND STREAMS, WHICH CARRY THEM ALL THE WAY TO THE OCEAN. AND THE SEA KEEPS COLLECTING IT LIKE A GIANT SOUP POT.

If water keeps flowing in, doesn't the salt get diluted?

YOU'D THINK SO! BUT HERE'S THE TWIST: WHEN SEAWATER EVAPORATES (THANKS TO THE SUN), THE WATER PART RISES INTO THE SKY TO FORM CLOUDS—BUT THE SALT STAYS BEHIND. THAT MEANS THE SALTY BITS JUST KEEP PILING UP.

Is it the same kind of salt we use on chips?

YES! SEA SALT IS A LOT LIKE THE SALT IN YOUR KITCHEN—ONLY IT HASN'T BEEN CLEANED OR CRUSHED. PEOPLE ACTUALLY MAKE SALT BY DRYING SEAWATER UNTIL THE WATER IS GONE AND ONLY THE CRYSTALS ARE LEFT.

Can the sea get too salty?

IN SOME PLACES, IT ALREADY HAS! THE DEAD SEA IS SO SALTY, YOU CAN FLOAT WITHOUT TRYING. BUT MOST OCEANS STAY JUST SALTY ENOUGH FOR SEA CREATURES TO LIVE COMFORTABLY.

Is it the wind's fault ?

YES—MOSTLY! WIND BLOWS ACROSS THE SURFACE OF THE WATER AND PUSHES IT INTO RIPPLES. THOSE RIPPLES GROW INTO BIGGER AND BIGGER WAVES. THAT'S WHY WINDY DAYS MAKE CHOPPY SEAS.

Do waves only happen when it's windy ?

NOT ALWAYS. THERE ARE OTHER WAVE-MAKERS TOO—LIKE THE MOON! ITS PULL ON THE EARTH MAKES THE SEA RISE AND FALL IN TIDES. IT'S A GENTLE TUG THAT MOVES A LOT OF WATER OVER TIME.

Why Do Waves Keep Moving?

What about really big waves?

SOME OF THE BIGGEST WAVES COME FROM UNDER THE SEA! WHEN THERE'S AN UNDERWATER EARTHQUAKE, IT CAN SHAKE THE WATER ABOVE IT,THOSE ARE CALLED TSUNAMIS, AND THEY'RE NOT LIKE REGULAR WAVES AT ALL.

Do waves ever get tired?

NOT REALLY. WAVES TRAVEL ACROSS THE OCEAN UNTIL THEY HIT SOMETHING—LIKE A BEACH,A BOAT, OR A REEF. SOME WAVES TAKE DAYS TO REACH SHORE. THEY RISE, ROLL, AND CRASH IN AN ENDLESS WATERY RHYTHM.

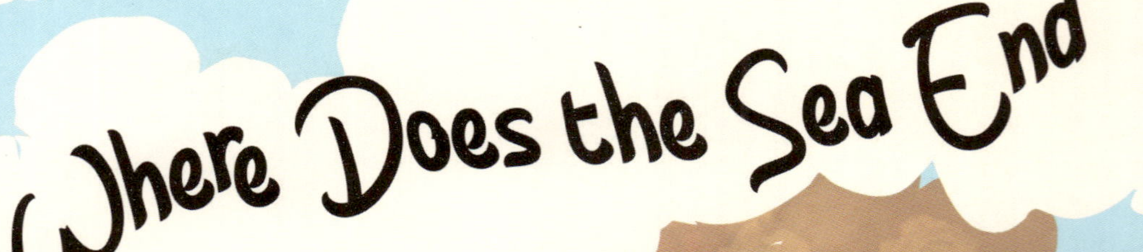

Is there a finish line somewhere?

NOT REALLY! THE SEA WRAPS ALL THE WAY AROUND THE EARTH. WE GIVE PARTS OF IT DIFFERENT NAMES—LIKE ATLANTIC OR PACIFIC—BUT IT'S ONE BIG CONNECTED OCEAN

Does the sea ever stop?

IT STOPS WHEN IT MEETS LAND—BUT THAT EDGEIS ALWAYS CHANGING. TIDES MAKE THE WATER MOVE IN AND OUT, SO THE SHORELINE WIGGLES FORWARD AND BACK LIKE A SLEEPY DANCER.

Can the sea sink into the ground?

A LITTLE!
THE SEA SOAKS INTO SAND AND ROCK BENEATH IT. IF YOU DIG A HOLE AT THE BEACH, YOU'LL SOON FIND WATER–BECAUSE THE SEA DOESN'T JUST SIT ON THE LAND. IT SEEPS INTO IT, LIKE A SNEAKY SPONGE.

Is there land under the sea too?

ABSOLUTELY!
UNDER THE WAVES, THE SEA FLOOR HAS MOUNTAINS, VALLEYS, VOLCANOES–EVEN CANYONS DEEPER THAN THE GRAND CANYON. IT'S A WHOLE WORLD WE BARELY SEE.

So, where does it end?

MAYBE IT DOESN'T. MAYBE THE SEA JUST KEEPS GOING–CHANGINGSHAPE, MAKING WAVES, HIDING TREASURES, AND WHISPERING SECRETS TO EVERY SHORE.

Why Is The Sea Blue?

Is the sea really blue or is it pretending?

THE SEA ISN'T BLUE ON ITS OWN. IT LOOKS BLUE BECAUSE OF HOW SUNLIGHT WORKS. WHEN LIGHT HITS THE WATER, MOST COLOURS GET ABSORBED. BLUE BOUNCES BACK-AND THAT'S WHAT WE SEE!

So if I scoop some up, it won't be blue?

RIGHT! A GLASS OF SEAWATER WILL LOOK CLEAR. IT ONLY LOOKS BLUE WHEN THERE'S LOTS OF WATER-LIKE IN THE OCEAN-BECAUSE THAT'S WHEN LIGHT AND WATER DO THEIR COLOUR DANCE.

What colour is the deepest sea?

IN THE DEEP OCEAN, WHERE SUNLIGHT CAN'T REACH, THE WATER IS A DARK, INKY BLUE—ALMOST BLACK. IT'S PEACEFUL, QUIET, AND MYSTERIOUS DOWN THERE.

Can the sea be other colours too?

YES! THE SEA CAN BE GREEN, GREY, BROWN, OR EVEN GOLD AT SUNSET. IF THERE'S ALGAE IN THE WATER, IT MIGHT TURN GREEN. IF THE SKY IS STORMY, IT MIGHT LOOK BLACK. IT'S LIKE A GIANT MIRROR REFLECTING WHATEVER'S AROUND IT.

What if the sky was purple - would the sea be purple too?

MAYBE! AT SUNSET, WHEN THE SKY TURNS PINK OR PURPLE, THE SEA OFTEN REFLECTS THOSE COLOURS TOO. IT'S ALWAYS WATCHING THE SKY AND SHOWING US WHAT IT SEES.

What Lives Deep, Deep Down ?

Is there anything down there at all ?

"YES! EVEN IN THE DARKEST, DEEPEST PARTS OF THE SEA—WHERE NO SUNLIGHT REACHES—THERE'S LIFE. STRANGE, GLOWING CREATURES. SQUID WITH GIANT EYES. FISH WITH SEE-THROUGH HEADS. THE DEEP SEA IS LIKE OUTER SPACE... BUT WETTER."

Is it cold down there ?

"VERY. IT CAN BE NEAR FREEZING. BUT DEEP-SEA ANIMALS HAVE ADAPTED. THEY MOVE SLOWLY, EAT RARELY, AND DON'T MIND THE PRESSURE, WHICH WOULD SQUISH A SUBMARINE!"

How do they live in the dark?
"SOME ANIMALS MAKE THEIROWN LIGHT! IT'S CALLED BIOLUMINESCENCE. IT HELPS THEM HUNT, HIDE, OR TALK TO OTHER DEEP-SEA CREATURES. THINK OF IT LIKE UNDERWATER FAIRY LIGHTS–EXCEPT THEY'RE ALIVE."
Do we know what's down there?
"NOT REALLY. WE'VE EXPLORED MORE OF THE MOON THAN THE OCEAN FLOOR. SCIENTISTS USE ROBOTS TO VISIT THE DEEP SEA, AND THEY KEEP FINDING WEIRD NEW CREATURES NO ONE'S EVER SEEN BEFORE."

Why Don't Fish Drown?

Don't they need air like we do?

YES!
BUT FISH DON'T BREATHE LIKE WE DO. THEY DON'T HAVE LUNGS—THEY HAVE GILLS. GILLS CAN PULL OXYGEN OUT OF WATER. AS WATER FLOWS THROUGH THEIR GILLS, THEY CATCH THE OXYGEN AND SEND IT INTO THEIR BLOOD.

Do whales have gills too?

NOPE!
WHALES ARE MAMMALS LIKE US. THEY HAVE LUNGS AND HAVE TO COME UP FOR AIR. THAT'S WHY THEY BLOW WATER FROM THEIR BLOWHOLES—IT'S THEM EXHALING! LIKE SAYING, "PHEW!"

So water has air in it?

IT DOES! TINY BUBBLES OF OXYGEN FLOAT IN WATER, EVEN THOUGH WE CAN'T SEE THEM. THAT'S HOW FISH, CRABS, AND EVEN SEA SNAILS STAY ALIVE UNDERWATER.

What happens if the water gets dirty?
IF WATER IS POLLUTED OR HAS TOO LITTLE OXYGEN, FISH CAN GET SICK—OR DIE. THAT'S WHY CLEAN WATER IS SO IMPORTANT FOR SEA LIFE.

Can the Sea Glow in the Dark?

Wait, can it really glow?

YES! IN SOME PLACES, THE SEA SPARKLES AT NIGHT. IT GLOWS BLUE-GREEN WHEN TINY CREATURES CALLED PLANKTON LIGHT UP. THEY GLOW WHEN THEY'RE MOVED—BY WAVES, BOATS, OR EVEN YOUR HANDS.

Can I make it glow myself?

SOMETIMES, YES! IF YOU SPLASH IN GLOWING WATER, IT MIGHT SPARKLE AROUND YOUR HANDS AND FEET. LIKE SWIMMING IN FAIRY DUST.

Where can I see it?

IN WARM PLACES LIKE THE MALDIVES, PUERTO RICO, OR SOME BEACHES IN INDIA, YOU CAN SEE GLOWING WATER. IT'S LIKE MAGIC—BUT IT'S SCIENCE!

Why do they glow?

IT'S THEIR WAY OF SAYING "DON'T EAT ME!" OR "HERE I AM!" IT'S CALLED BIOLUMINESCENCE, AND IT'S KIND OF LIKE FIREFLIES IN WATER.

Why Are Some Seas Warm and Some Cold?

Is the sea like a bathtub?

SORT OF!
THE SUN HEATS THE TOP OF THE OCEAN, SO PLACES NEAR THE EQUATOR (LIKE INDIA, AFRICA, AND AUSTRALIA) HAVE WARM SEAS.
PLACES NEAR THE POLES (LIKE ANTARCTICA) ARE ICY COLD.

So the Sun makes the difference?

MOSTLY, YES. BUT OCEAN CURRENTS ALSO PLAY A PART. WARM WATER TRAVELS FROM THE EQUATOR TOWARD COLDER PLACES, AND COLD WATER TRAVELS BACK DOWN. IT'S LIKE THE SEA HAS CONVEYOR BELTS!

Can the same sea be warm and cold?

YES!
SURFACE WATER CAN BE WARM, WHILE DEEP WATER STAYS COLD. IT'S LIKE A LAYERED OCEAN CAKE!

What's it like in the cold sea ?

CHILLY!
ANIMALS THERE HAVE
THICK BLUBBER OR FURRY COATS.
BUT EVEN ICY SEAS ARE
FULL OF LIFE–LIKE
PENGUINS, WHALES,
AND ICE FISH.

Do Mermaids Really Exist?

So they're not real ... but they are magical?

EXACTLY!
EVEN IF THEY DON'T SWIM IN REAL OCEANS, THEY LIVE IN OUR STORIES—AND MAYBE IN OUR IMAGINATION TOO.

Where did the idea come from?

LONG AGO, SAILORS MIGHT HAVE SEEN MANATEES OR DUGONGS AND THOUGHT THEY LOOKED LIKE PEOPLE FROM FAR AWAY. THAT'S WHERE MERMAID LEGENDS BEGAN.

Are they in every culture?

YES! IN AFRICA, THERE'S MAMI WATA. IN JAPAN, THERE ARE NINGYO. DIFFERENT PLACES HAVE THEIR OWN SEA SPIRITS AND MERMAID-LIKE MYTHS.

I saw one in a book! Could it be real?

MERMAIDS ARE PART OF MANY SEA STORIES, FROM ANCIENT SAILORS TO FAIRYTALES. THEY'RE HALF-HUMAN, HALF-FISH—BUT NO, SCIENTISTS HAVE NEVER FOUND ONE.

Why Do Crabs Walk Sideways?

Can't they just walk straight?

CRABS HAVE JOINTS IN THEIR LEGS THAT MAKE IT EASIER TO MOVE SIDEWAYS. IT'S LIKE HOW SOME TOYS ROLL BETTER IN ONE DIRECTION—THEY'RE BUILT THAT WAY!

Do all crabs walk the same way?

NO! SOME CRABS, LIKE FIDDLER CRABS, CAN CLIMB AND DIG. OTHERS, LIKE COCONUT CRABS, CAN EVEN CLIMB TREES!

Is sideways walking faster?

FOR CRABS, YES! THEIR LEGS MOVE LIKE PADDLES, HELPING THEM ZIP ACROSS SAND OR ROCKS IN A SCUTTLE.

What's with the claws?

BIG CLAWS HELP CRABS DEFEND THEMSELVES, CRACK SHELLS, AND SHOW OFF. SOME HAVE ONE BIG CLAW AND ONE SMALL ONE–LIKE A CRAB-SIZED SWORD AND SPOON!

What's Hiding in a Rock Pool?

What's a rock pool?

IT'S A TINY WORLD LEFT BEHIND WHEN THE TIDE GOES OUT! WATER GETS TRAPPED IN HOLES AND DIPS IN ROCKS, FORMING LITTLE HOMES FOR SEA CREATURES.

Who lives there?

STARFISH, SEA ANEMONES, CRABS, SNAILS, TINY FISH, AND SOMETIMES EVEN OCTOPUSES! THEY STAY COOL AND SAFE UNTIL THE TIDE COMES BACK.

Is it like a sea zoo ?

KIND OF! BUT IT'S NOT JUST FOR LOOKING. ROCK POOL CREATURES ARE DELICATE. YOU CAN WATCH THEM—BUT BEST NOT TO POKE.

Can I explore one near me ?

YES—IF YOU'RE NEAR THE COAST, YOU MIGHT FIND ONE. WEAR SHOES, GO SLOW, AND LOOK CLOSELY. IT'S LIKE A SECRET TREASURE HUNT.

Why Do Whales Sing?

Wait! they sing? Like music?

YES! HUMPBACK WHALES SING LONG, BEAUTIFUL SONGS UNDERWATER. THEIR SOUND CAN TRAVEL FOR HUNDREDS OF KILOMETRES!

What are they singing about?

SCIENTISTS THINK THEY SING TO ATTRACT MATES OR TALK TO EACH OTHER. IT'S LIKE WHALE RADIO–WITH RHYTHMS, PATTERNS, EVEN VERSES.

Can other animals hear it?

YES! SOME FISH, DOLPHINS, AND EVEN BOATS CAN PICK IT UP. TO WHALES, THE OCEAN IS FILLED WITH SOUND.

Can we hear it too?

YES—YOU CAN LISTEN TO WHALE SONGS ONLINE. THEY SOUND SPOOKY, DEEP, AND WONDERFUL—LIKE THE OCEAN HUMMING A LULLABY.

What Happens During a Storm at Sea?

Do fish get scared?

NOT REALLY. MOST SEA CREATURES DIVE DEEPER WHERE IT'S CALM. THE STORM MOSTLY DANCES ON THE SURFACE, NOT DEEP BELOW.

What about the waves?

THEY GET HUGE! WIND PUSHES WATER INTO BIG, CRASHING WAVES. SHIPS ROCK, SEAGULLS HIDE, AND SEAFOAM FLIES LIKE WHIPPED CREAM.

Is it dangerous?

IT CAN BE. THAT'S WHY SAILORS CHECK WEATHER BEFORE THEY SAIL. BUT THE OCEAN IS USED TO STORMS—IT'S BEEN THROUGH MILLIONS OF THEM.

What does the sea look like after ?
SOMETIMES QUIET.
SOMETIMES WILD.
THE STORM CHURNS UP NEW
THINGS—SEAWEED, SHELLS,
AND SECRETS. THE SEA
NEVER STAYS THE SAME FOR LONG.

Can We Ever Run Out of Sea?

Could it dry up?

THE SEA IS PART OF THE WATER CYCLE. IT EVAPORATES, TURNS INTO CLOUDS, RAINS BACK DOWN, AND FLOWS INTO RIVERS AND BACK TO SEA. SO IT ALWAYS COMES BACK!

But what about pollution?

THAT'S A REAL DANGER. TRASH, OIL, AND CHEMICALS CAN HURT SEA LIFE. WE WON'T "RUN OUT" OF WATER—BUT WE COULD HARM THE SEA IF WE'RE NOT CAREFUL.

Can we protect it?

YES! PICKING UP LITTER, USING LESS PLASTIC, AND LEARNING ABOUT THE OCEAN HELPS. EVEN SMALL ACTIONS CAN MAKE BIG WAVES OF CHANGE.

So will the sea stay safe?

ONLY IF WE TAKE CARE OF IT. THE SEA GIVES US SO MUCH—FOOD, AIR, BEAUTY. IT'S OUR TURN TO GIVE SOMETHING BACK.

Let's Wonder Some More

A mini quiz :

WHICH ANIMAL SINGS ?

____

WHAT GLOWS IN THE SEA ?

____

WHAT MAKES WAVES ?

____

The sea is waiting for you – will you explore it with care !